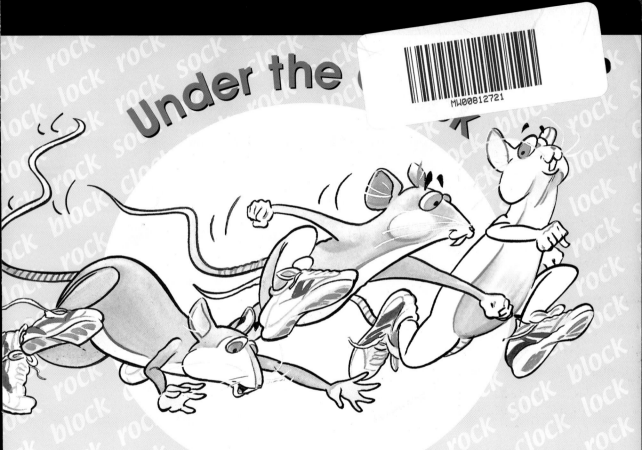

Under the

Written by Michele Paul
Illustrated by Brent Putze

Under the clock
and over the block.

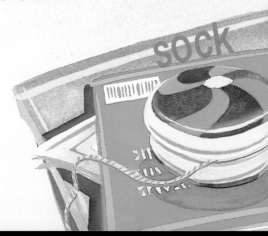

2

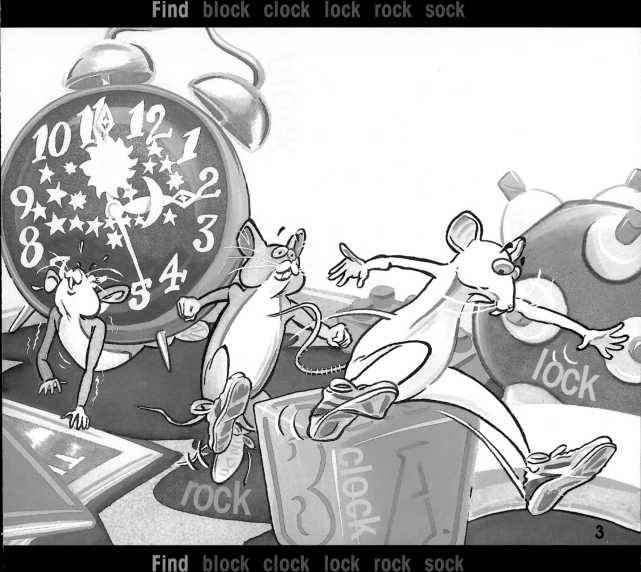

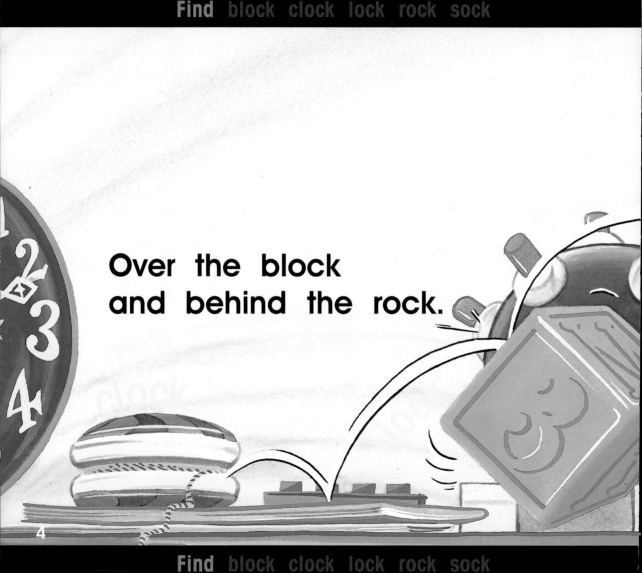

Over the block
and behind the rock.

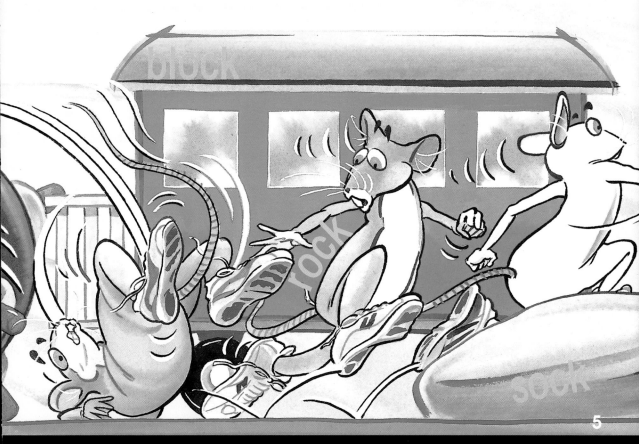

5

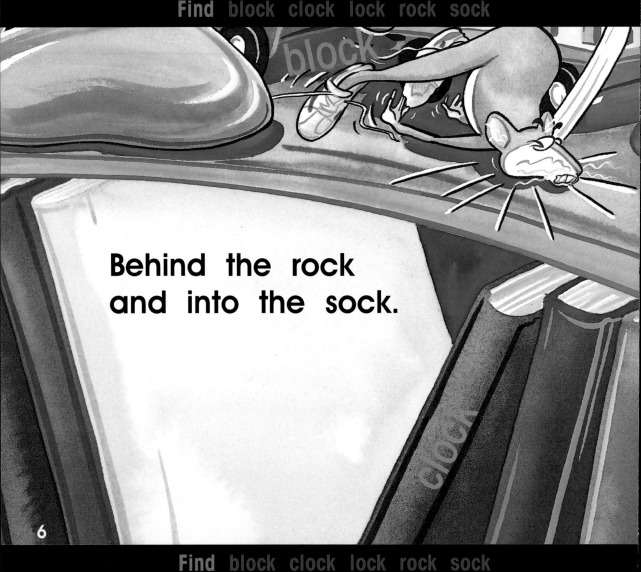

Behind the rock
and into the sock.

6

7

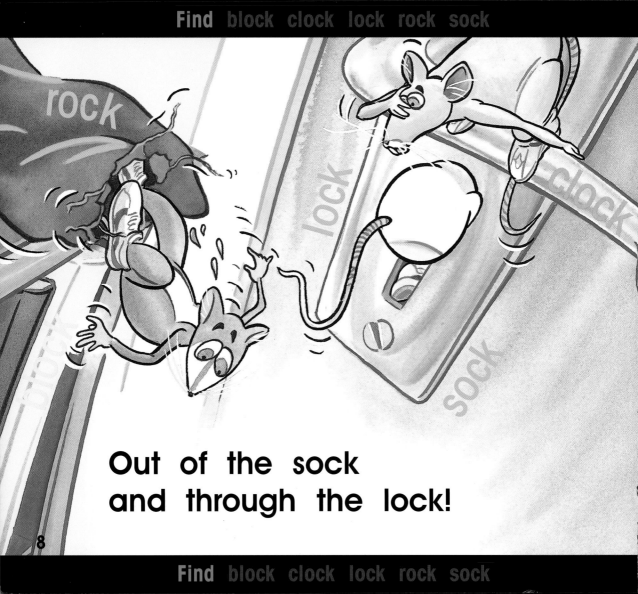

Out of the sock
and through the lock!

8